It's Valentine's Day!

by Richard Sebra

BUMBA BOOKS™

LERNER PUBLICATIONS ◆ MINNEAPOLIS

Note to Educators:

Throughout this book, you'll find critical thinking questions. These can be used to engage young readers in thinking critically about the topic and in using the text and photos to do so.

Lerner Publications Company
A division of Lerner Publishing Group, Inc.
241 First Avenue North
Minneapolis, MN 55401 USA

For reading levels and more information, look up this title at www.lernerbooks.com.

Library of Congress Cataloging-in-Publication Data

Names: Sebra, Richard, 1984- author.
Title: It's Valentine's Day! / by Richard Sebra.
Description: Minneapolis : Lerner Publications, [2017] | Series: Bumba Books — It's a Holiday! | Includes bibliographical references and index. | Audience: Ages: 4–8. | Audience: Grades: K to Grade 3.
Identifiers: LCCN 2016018668 (print) | LCCN 2016028639 (ebook) | ISBN 9781512425628 (lb : alk. paper) | ISBN 9781512429206 (pb : alk. paper) | ISBN 9781512427417 (eb pdf)
Subjects: LCSH: Valentine's Day—Juvenile literature.
Classification: LCC GT492 .S43 2017 (print) | LCC GT492 (ebook) | DDC 394.2618—dc23

LC record available at https://lccn.loc.gov/2016018668

Manufactured in the United States of America
1 – VP – 12/31/16

Expand learning beyond the printed book. Download free, complementary educational resources for this book from our website, www.lernerresource.com.

Table of
Contents

Valentine's Day

Valentine's Day is a holiday.

We celebrate it on February 14.

What is another holiday that is in February?

This holiday is about love.

People show love to those they

care about.

People spend time

with loved ones.

Someone you love is

called your valentine.

Valentines are also greetings.

People give valentines.

These notes say how people feel.

What might you write on your valentines?

I make a box for my valentines.

I will bring it to a party.

Valentine's Day colors are red, pink, and white.

People wear red.

They give red, pink, and white flowers.

Hearts are symbols of love.

They are symbols of

Valentine's Day.

People give candy too.

Chocolates come in boxes

shaped like hearts.

What else could you give your valentine?

Valentine's Day is a day to

show love.

Who will you give a valentine to?

Valentine's Day Symbols

hearts

flowers

valentines

chocolates

Picture Glossary

holiday

a day to celebrate

symbols

objects or pictures that stand for something else

valentine

someone you love

valentines

gifts or greeting cards you give to loved ones

Index

Read More

McGee, Randel. *Paper Crafts for Valentine's Day.* Berkeley Heights, NJ: Enslow Elementary, 2015.

Pettiford, Rebecca. *Valentine's Day.* Minneapolis: Jump!, 2016.

Sebra, Richard. *It's Halloween!* Minneapolis: Lerner Publications, 2017.

Photo Credits